Here's wha about tl

As a fresh graduate, this book has helped me earn my first internship. I can never forget thanking you guys for it. - *Deepesh Chabria*

This book was my first buy. I am so impressed; I have the complete set for my reference. It's really handy!
- *Tom Wheat*

You guys have covered every important interview question in this book. Also includes the LINQ and other latest stuff. Good book! - *Victoria Darner*

I bought your .NET Framework before buying this copy. When are you going to release the C# book? Eagerly waiting! - *Nate Ruppel*

Super book. Covers everything one would need. But beware; you should be good at the basics before going through this one! This is a perfect LMR (Last Minute Revision Book)! - *Amy Crunkilton*

This page is intentionally left blank

ASP.NET
Interview Questions
You'll Most Likely Be Asked

Job Interview Questions Series

 **Vibrant Publishers**

www.vibrantpublishers.com

ASP.NET Interview Questions
You'll Most Likely Be Asked

© 2011, By Vibrant Publishers, USA. All rights reserved. No part of this publication may be reproduced or distributed in any form or by any means, or stored in a database or retrieval system, without the prior permission of the publisher.

ISBN-10: 1453895078
ISBN-13: 978-14-53895-07-8

Library of Congress Control Number: 2010939498

This publication is designed to provide accurate and authoritative information in regard to the subject matter covered. The author has made every effort in the preparation of this book to ensure the accuracy of the information. However, information in this book is sold without warranty either expressed or implied. The Author or the Publisher will not be liable for any damages caused or alleged to be caused either directly or indirectly by this book.

The publisher wishes to thank Pasnicu Oana (Romania) for her invaluable inputs to this edition.

Vibrant Publishers books are available at special quantity discount for sales promotions, or for use in corporate training programs. For more information please write to **bulkorders@vibrantpublishers.com**

Please email feedback / corrections (technical, grammatical or spelling) to **spellerrors@vibrantpublishers.com**

To access the complete catalogue of Vibrant Publishers, visit **www.vibrantpublishers.com**

ASP.NET Questions

Review these typical interview questions and think about how you would answer them. Read the answers listed; you will find best possible answers along with strategies and suggestions.

This page is intentionally left blank

INTRODUCTION TO ASP.NET

1: How many types of ASP.NET are currently released?

Answer:

The current version of ASP.NET is at 4.0; previous versions include 1, 1.1, 2.0 and 3.5. The current version is more concentrated on AJAX and LINQ. Version 3.0 of ASP.NET does not exist.

2: What does ASP.NET 2.0 improve over the previous version?

Answer:

ASP.NET 2.0 improves by adding new features such as: master pages, new controls, themes, security, profiles and more.

3: What does ASP.NET AJAX do?

Answer:

ASP.NET AJAX gives the user a great deal of options that help integrate AJAX into normal ASP.NET pages. It ensures that users can write more powerful JavaScript.

4: What is LINQ and what does it do?

Answer:

LINQ means Language Integrated Query and is an extension to the C# and VB languages. It allows for writing of these languages codes that manipulate in-memory data just like querying a database.

5: Do current web browsers support ASP.NET 3.5? What is the role of ASP.NET in web development?

Answer:

Yes, Current browser versions fully support ASP.NET 3.5(IE 5, Opera 7.6, Safari 1.2 and Firefox 1.0). ASP.NET is designed to provide a client callback feature that handles some of the work web browsers should handle.

6: Is ASP.NET 3.5 a full ASP.NET version?

Answer:

No ASP.NET 3.5 is designed to add features over the 2.0 version and the most important ones are: CLR and WCF. New 3.5 version list of important assemblies consists of:

a) System – core;

b) Data.Linq;

c) data.DataSetExtension;

d) Xml.Linq and

e) Web.Extensions – dll.

7: How do you add ASP.NET into a web site?

Answer:

After creating a new web site you can add ASP.NET by going to the option menu, selecting add new item; you then select web form and enter the value FirstPage.aspx.

WEB FORMS and

OBJECTS

8: What are web forms and what do they do?

Answer:

Web forms allow the creation of a web based application that uses the same interface as Windows applications.

9: What is page processing?

Answer:

Page processing allows ASP.NET to execute the web server on the server by a technique called postback. It also enables ASP to create a seamless user experience where web applications are stateless.

10: How are controls handled in ASP.NET?

Answer:

Controls are placed in a <form> tag that is marked with the runat="server" attribute/ thus allowing the user to work on the server side of the application.

11: What is the ASP.NET event model?

Answer:

ASP.NET provides a change to the linear processing model because of its event driven model. By providing, each event handler with a discrete method, the page code becomes organized and clean.

12: How do the events in ASP.NET function?

Answer:

The events allow ASP.NET to create pages and control objects so that the newly created page can run smooth; it also triggers a postback and intercepts the returned page recreating the page objects; it then checks the operations triggered by the postback and finally renders the HTML page and returns it to the client.

13: What is the view state mechanism in ASP.NET?

Answer:

To deal with the limitations of HTML, ASP has an integrated state serialization mechanism. It means that properties of a certain page that get changed enable ASP to make notes and keep track of them.

14: Does ASP.NET follow the rules of XHTML?

Answer:

Yes. The core ASP controls follow the XHTML rules and to make sure the page is compliant with XHMTL the users have to make sure the static content they add follows these rules.

15: How does the user code initialize?

Answer:

It is done by using the Page.Load event in the stage of processing of a page. This event always sets off no matter if the page is being requested for the first time or part of a postback.

16: Does ASP.NET include validation controls?

Answer:

Yes it does. These controls fire before a page is loaded but before the actual events take place. By having the validation controls self-sufficient ASP.NET does not make it mandatory for the user to respond to them.

17: What is the Response object in ASP.NET?

Answer:

The Response object is an instance of the System.Web.HttpResponse class and is the server's response to a class. It provides important functionality: cookie features and the Redirect () method.

18: What is the Server object?

Answer:

The Server object is an instance of the System.Web.HttpServerUtility class and it provides miscellaneous methods and properties that help the web server.

19: What is the User object?

Answer:

The User object shows information about the user making a

request to a web server and it allows the users to see the user's role membership by implementing the System.Security.Principal.IPrincipal.

20: What is the Trace object?

Answer:

The trace object is a general tracing tool that allows the writing of information into a log scoped at the page level. It also shows a multitude of miscellaneous information that is grouped into several sections.

SERVER CONTROLS, OBJECTS and METHODS

21: What are server controls in ASP.NET?

Answer:

Server controls are classes that represent the visual elements on the web form and are a fundamental part of ASP.NET.

22: How many types of server controls does ASP.NET allow?

Answer:

There are four main types of server controls and these are:

    a) HTML server controls,

    b) Web controls,

    c) Rich controls and

    d) Validation controls.

23: What is the HTML server control class and what does it do?

Answer:

This class derives from the base class of the HTMLControl and is used for creating instances of the HTML servers that the user can set properties to.

24: What is the WebControl class and what does it do?

Answer:

The Web control class is derived from the WebControl base class and it enables important features such as automatic postback and provides the user with a more consistent model than the servers of HTML.

25: What is the Page class and what does it do?

Answer:

The Page class is found in the System.Web.UI namespace and is the instance for all web forms. Every web form that the user creates has a great amount of functionality right out of the box: every core class derives from the System.Web.UI.Page.

26: What is the Session object?

Answer:

The Session object is a System.Web.SessionState.HttpSessionState class instance. It was designed to store types of user data that must persist between requests of web pages.

27: What is the Application object?

Answer:

The Application object is an instance of System.Web.SessionState.HttpSessionState class and was designed as a name/value dictionary of data, but this data is specific to the whole application.

28: What is the Cache object?

Answer:

The Cache object is an instance belonging to the System.Web.Caching.Cache class which, like the Application object, stores global information providing a more scalable storage mechanism.

29: What is the Request object?

Answer:

The Request object belongs to the System.Web.HttpRequest

class and represents the values of the HTTP request that made the web page load. It contains all the information that the client has sent.

30: What is the Response object?

Answer:

The Response object is an instance belonging to the System.Web.HttpResponse class and is the response that the web server provides to a request from the client.

31: What is a Server object?

Answer:

The Server object belongs to the System.Web.HttpServerUtility class and provides the user a lot of helper methods and properties.

32: What is the Transfer() method?

Answer:

The Transfer() method is the easiest and quickest way to

redirect the user to another page in an application without the use of a round-trip.

33: What is the MapPath() method?

Answer:

The MapPath() method is a method of the Server object that converts the relative paths of a web application into a physical path.

34: What is the HtmlEncode() method?

Answer:

The HtmlEncode() method is useful for retrieving values from a database while making sure the text has validity in HTML.

35: What is the User object?

Answer:

The User object represents information about the user that makes a request to a web server allowing for a full test of the user's membership. It implements the

System.Security.Principal.IPrincipal class.

36: What is the Trace object?

Answer:

The Trace object is part of the System.Web.TraceContext class and is considered to be a multi, general purpose tracing tool: it allows for writing information into a log that is scoped at the page level.

ASP.NET

DATA BINDING

37: What does Data binding do in ASP.NET?

Answer:

Data binding allows the binding of retrieved data objects to one or more web controls showing the data automatically; it is often used in conjunction with data source controls.

38: What are data source controls?

Answer:

Data source controls allow the user to define a declarative link between his page and a data source. After configuration they also allow for connection to the web controls at the time of design.

39: What is Basic Data Binding?

Answer:

Basic Data Binding is a feature that allows for association of a data source with a control having that control display the data automatically. It is declarative and in NO form programmatic.

40: What does the Single Value Binding do?

Answer:

Single value binding allows for the binding of controls to a data binding expression. The expression is inserted in the .aspx markup portion of a page and it is closed with the <% # and %> delimiters.

41: What does the Repeated Value Binding do?

Answer:

The repeated value binding allows for the binding of a whole list of information to a control with the list of information being represented by a data object that encases a collection of items. The items can either be a collection of custom objects or a row collection.

42: What does Data Source Controls comprise of?

Answer:

Data Source Controls includes any control that implements the IDataSource interface. These controls are:

a) SqlDataSource,

b) ObjectDataSource,

c) AccesDataSource,

d) XmlDataSource, and,

e) SiteMapDataSource.

43: What does the SqlDataSource do?

Answer:

The SqlDataSource is a database connection that uses an ADO.NET provider. It needs a generic way to create the Connection, Command and DataReader objects it needs.

44: What does the ObjectDataSource do?

Answer:

It allows for creation of a declarative link between the controls of a web page and the data access component that updates the data.

DATA CONTROLS and

CACHING

45: What is the GridView control?

Answer:

The GridView is a grid control that shows data in a basic grid that is made of row and columns and it is capable of using features such as selection, paging or editing.

46: What is the ListView control?

Answer:

The ListView control is introduced in ASP.NET 3.5 and it designed solely for replacing the Repeater control. It is a data bound control that renders its content based on templates defined by the user.

47: What does the DetailsView do in ASP.NET?

Answer:

The DetailsView control is made to show a single record at a time and places each piece of information in a separate row of a table.

48: What does the FormView do in ASP.NET?

Answer:

The FormView control provides a template only control for displaying and editing a single record; it also matches the model of the TemplateField in the GridView closely thus allowing for content available in GridView to be placed in FormView.

49: What is Caching?

Answer:

Caching is a technique of storing an in-memory copy of information that is expensive to create; it is also used because of its abilities to enhance performance and scalability.

50: How many types of caching can we find in ASP.NET?

Answer:

There are two types of caching:

    a) output caching and — *Copy of HTML Page in Memory*

    b) data caching; with two more types of cache building on

these models: fragment and data source caching.

51: What does output caching do?

Answer:

Output caching renders the HTML so that when the same page is requested again the control objects are not created again and no code executes but instead serves the cached HTML.

52: What does data caching do?

Answer:

Data caching adds items that are too expensive to create to a special built-in collection object. It is thread safe and items in cache are automatically removed.

53: How can portions of a web page be cached?

Answer:

Sometimes a page cannot be entirely cached so there is an option of caching just a portion of a web page with fragment caching and post-cache substitution.

54: How can fragment caching be implemented?

Answer:

Fragment caching can be implemented by creating a user control for the portion that the user wants to cache and then adding the OutputCache directive to the user control.

55: What is Post-Cache substitution?

Answer:

Post-cache substitution is useful when the page as a whole is cached, but fragments within the page are dynamic. With post-cache substitution, you can configure the page to be cached, but mark individual sections of the page as not cacheable.

56: What does cache configuration do?

Answer:

Cache configuration allows for various details of ASP.NET to be configured through the web.config and it is intended to be used for easier debugging.

57: What does cache priority do and what is it used for?

Answer:

Cache priority is used for adding an item to the cache; the priority has an effect only if ASP.NET needs to perform cache scavenging by removing cached items early for the lack of memory.

STREAMS and

FILES

58: What do DirectoryInfo and FileInfo classes do?

Answer:

They are mirror classes of the Directory and File classes and they ease the walking of directory and file relationships by providing a combination of properties and methods.

59: What does the DriveInfo do?

Answer:

The DriveInfo class is used to retrieve information about a certain drive on the user's computer and it is usually used for retrieving the total amount of used and free space.

60: How can File Version Information be retrieved?

Answer:

File Version Information can be retrieved by using the static GetVersionInfo() method of the System.Diagnostics.FileVersionInfo class.

61: What does the Path class do?

Answer:

The Path class provides static helper methods that perform common path manipulation tasks by using the System.IO.Path class.

62: What are streams in ASP.NET?

Answer:

Streams are data in the memory buffer that is retrieved over a network connection and from or written to a file.

63: How can text files be implemented with ASP.NET?

Answer:

Text files can be written and read by using the StreamWritter and the StreamReaderr classes in the System.IO namespace and by passing the underlying stream as a constructor argument.

64: How can binary files be implemented in ASP.NET?

Answer:

Binary files can be implemented by creating a new

BinaryWriter class. The class constructor accepts a stream that can then be created by hand or retrieved using the File.OpenWrite() method.

65: How can files be uploaded into ASP.NET?

Answer:

Files can be uploaded by using one of the two controls incorporated into ASP.NET. They are HtmlInputFile and FileUpload.

66: What happens when a file bigger than 4MB is uploaded into ASP.NET?

Answer:

Uploading a file bigger than 4MB results in a runtime error; this can be modified by using the maxRequestLength attribute in the application's web.config file.

67: What does compression do in ASP.NET?

Answer:

Compression allows the user to compress data written to any file with the support of the GZipStream and DeflateStream classes.

68: How is compression used in ASP.NET?

Answer:

To use compression the user has to wrap the real stream with a compression stream, be it either a FileStream or a MemoryStream.

69: What does Serialization do in ASP.NET?

Answer:

Serialization is a high level model that is built into .NET and is a technique of storing data into a file. It allows for converting an entire live object into a series of bytes that are then written into a stream object.

LINQ

70: What is LINQ?

Answer:

LINQ is a set of language extensions that allow the performing of queries; it can define keywords that the user uses to build expressions.

71: How do LINQ expressions work?

Answer:

LINQ expressions are similar to SQL queries but the order that the classes have are rearranged. All expressions must have a form clause that shows the data source and a select clause which shows the data the user wishes to retrieve.

72: What do Grouping and Aggregation do in LINQ?

Answer:

Grouping allows the user the condensation of a large set of information into a smaller set of summary results while the aggregate function allows for a calculation with the data in the group to be performed.

73: What are extension methods in LINQ?

Answer:

Extension methods allow the user to define a method in one class but call it as it was defined in a different class. They are defined in the System.Linq.Enumerable class.

74: What happens when LINQ to DataSet is used?

Answer:

Using LINQ to DataSet the user uses the same expressions used to query collections of objects. The Field<T> method is used which is provided by the DataRowExtension class in the System.

75: What are Typed DataSets in LINQ?

Answer:

Typed DataSets are used for solving the limitations of the DataSet eliminating the use of Field<T> and AsEnumerable() methods, resulting in more readable expressions.

76: What does using LINQ to SQL result in?

Answer:

LINQ expressions are used to query data in SQL server databases. They are translated into SQL queries and it then executes these queries when the user needs the data.

77: What does DataContext do?

Answer:

The DataContext class incorporates all the core functionality needed to work with LINQ to SQL and is a starting point for working with LINQ to SQL.

78: What does LinqDataSource do?

Answer:

LinqDataSource control is used to retrieve and bind data in the code automatically allowing the user to skip writing of SQL queries manually.

XML in ASP.NET

79: What is XML?

Answer:

XML is a set of guidelines defined by W3C that describe a set of structured data in plain text. It is a meta language that allows for the creation of other mark up languages.

80: What are the advantages of using XML?

Answer:

XML in its current state is a very powerful language that allows an easy adoption by different companies. It is extensible and flexible and has a large array of tools programmers can use.

81: What is a Schema in XML?

Answer:

A Schema is a formal document that is created with the sole purpose of stating rules of a custom markup language. It lists the logical rules that the user defines for a particular type of used data.

82: How can a XML file be written?

Answer:

There are two ways of writing files in XML: one way is to build a document using the XmlDocument or XDocument classes and the second way is to write a document directly to a stream by using the XmlTextWriter.

83: What are the strategies of reading XML files?

Answer:

There are two ways of reading XML content: one way is to read it in one go with XmlDocument, XPathNavigator or XDocument classes and the second way is to skim through the content node by node by using XmlTextReader.

84: What is a node in XML?

Answer:

A node is the basis of an XML file and it can either be an element, attribute, comment or a value in an element.

85: What does the XPath Navigator class do?

Answer:

The XPath Navigator is similar to the XmlDocument class in that it loads all the information in the memory allowing then the user to move through the nodes.

86: What does the XDocument do and what is its function?

Answer:

The XDocument is used for managing in-memory XML and constructing content with clean code.

87: How can XML content be read with XDocument?

Answer:

XML content can be read by using the XDocument.Load() method. This can be used to read documents from a file, URI or stream. Users can also use the XDocument.Parse() method to load XML content from a string.

88: How can XML content be searched?

Answer:

This can be achieved by using the GetElementsByTagName() method for simple scenarios or the XPath language for sophisticated cases.

89: How is XML content transforming achieved?

Answer:

XML content transforming is achieved by using XSL for creating Stylesheets. These are special documents that are used to convert XML documents into other types of documents.

90: What does XML Control do?

Answer:

The XML control displays the result of an XSL transformation in a discrete part of a page.

91: What is the purpose of using XSLT?

Answer:

XSLT is used to ready the XML data for display in a

hierarchical control such as the TreeView.

USER CONTROLS

92: What are user controls in .NET?

Answer:

User controls is a small section in a page that includes static HTML code and also web server controls that can be reused in multiple pages across a single application.

93: What are custom server controls in .NET?

Answer:

Custom server controls are classes that that generate HTML code programmatically and are precompiled in DLL assemblies.

94: What do user controls comprise of?

Answer:

User controls are composed of a series of user interface portions with control tags and can contain almost everything a web page can.

95: How can a user control be created?

Answer:

A user control can be created in Visual Studio by selecting Website, scrolling to Add New Item and choosing the Web User Control template.

96: How can code be added to a user control?

Answer:

Code can be added in a user control by using a <script> block in the .ascx file or by using separate .cs code behind file method.

97: How are dynamic user controls added?

Answer:

To add dynamic user controls, the user must first add user controls when the Page.Load event fires, then use container and placeholder controls and finally give the user control a unique name setting ID property.

THEMES in ASP.NET

98: What are themes in ASP.NET?

Answer:

Themes are features that allow the user to define formatting details of different types of controls and then reuse these formats in multiple pages. Entire websites can be customized with these themes just by modifying the theme definition.

99: What are master pages in ASP.NET?

Answer:

Master pages are features that enable the reuse of page templates ensuring that all the website pages have the same design.

100: How can a Stylesheet be created?

Answer:

A Stylesheet can be created by choosing Website – Add New Item in Visual Studio.

101: What are Stylesheets used for?

Answer:

Stylesheets are used for defining a large array of rules. They are typically used for defining a website's user interface formatting.

102: How are Stylesheet rules applied?

Answer:

First of all a webpage has to be linked to a Stylesheet by adding a <link> in the <head> section of a page which references the file with styles the user wants to use and then static HTML element must be bind to the user's control rules.

103: Where are themes placed in a web application?

Answer:

Themes are placed in a user created folder named App_Themes that has to be inside the top level directory of the web application.

104: How can a Stylesheet be used as part of a theme?

Answer:

To use a Stylesheet in a theme the user has to first add the Stylesheet to the theme folder; this allows ASP.NET to search the folder for all .css files binding them to all pages that use that theme.

105: What are HTML frames?

Answer:

HTML frames is a tool of HTML that allows the display of more than one page in a browser window at once with the disadvantage that the code on each page must be independent because each page is retrieved through a separate request to the server.

WEBSITES and NAVIGATION

106: What is the MultiView Control?

Answer:

MultiView is the simpler form of the view controls and it is used to give users a mean of declaring multiple views that are displayed one at a time; it is created using the <asp:MultiView> tag to the .aspx page file.

107: What is the Wizard control?

Answer:

Wizard control is the more advanced version of MultiView control that supports showing several views at any given time and it also includes some customizable behavior like navigation buttons or sidebars.

108: What is XmlSiteMapProvider?

Answer:

XmlSiteMapProvider is a single site map provider that is able to retrieve site map information from and XML file.

109: What is SiteMapPath?

Answer:

SiteMapPath is a navigation control that shows the user's current location allowing him to navigate back to a higher level using links.

110: How can URL mapping be achieved?

Answer:

URL mapping is done in the <urlMappings> section of the web.config file by supplying two strings of information: the URL and the new URL destination.

111: What is the TreeView control?

Answer:

TreeView control is one of the most powerful navigation controls available in ASP.NET. Aside from rendering tree views it also allows for the filling of portions of the tree on demand.

112: What does the TreeNode do?

Answer:

The TreeNode is an object that provides navigation properties such as ChildNodes and Parent nodes. TreeNode has an associated piece of text that is displayed in the tree.

113: How many modes does TreeNode have?

Answer:

TreeNode has two types of modes:

a) Selection mode: This mode posts back the message and starts the TreeView.SelectedNodeChanged event.

b) Navigation mode: This mode enables the navigation to a new page by clicking a node. Navigation mode does not trigger the SelectNodeChange event.

114: What does the Menu Control do?

Answer:

The Menu control is an advanced control that supports hierarchical data. Its Menu can be bound to a data source or it can be filled manually by using the MenuItems class.

115: What does the MenuItem class do?

Answer:

MenuItem is similar to the TreeNode class but not as powerful and it allows setting images and specifying a target link.

SECURITY in ASP.NET

116: What is Authentication in ASP.NET?

Answer:

Authentication is the process of discovering a user's identity and ensuring the authenticity of this identity.

117: How do users prove their identity?

Answer:

First the user must provide his credentials to prove his identity and once it is verified the user is now able to go to different areas of the site.

118: How many types of authentications does ASP.NET provide?

Answer:

ASP supports four types of authentication:
- a) Windows authentication process,
- b) Form authentication process,
- c) Passport authentication process and
- d) Custom authentication process.

119: What is Impersonation?

Answer:

Impersonation is the process of executing code on behalf of another user. Impersonation can be avoided by giving each application different permissions or by using existing Windows permissions.

120: What is Authorization?

Answer:

Authorization is a process of determining the rights assigned to an authenticated user and grants them or denies them access to a specific part or even the whole website.

121: What is Confidentiality?

Answer:

Confidentiality is the process of ensuring that data cannot by viewed by unauthorized users while it is being transmitted over a stored data store.

122: What is Integrity?

Answer:

Integrity is the process of ensuring that no one can change the data that is transmitted (and during the process of transmitting) over a network.

123: What is Encryption?

Answer:

Encryption is the process of making data unreadable by other users. It is a separate feature from Authentication and Impersonation and it can be used in conjunction with these features or on its own.

124: How is Authentication handled in ASP.NET?

Answer:

Authentication is implemented thru HTTP modules with the ability of allowing the user to choose which module to use with the <authentication> element in the web.config file.

125: How many modules does ASP.NET use?

Answer:

ASP.NET has three core modules that it provides:

a) FormsAuthenticationModule

b) WindowsAuthenticationModule and

c) PassportAuthenticationModule.

126: What does FormsAuthenticationModule do?

Answer:

FormsAuthenticationModule uses forms of authentication that allows the user to design his own login pages but rely on ASP.NET role information using encrypted cookies.

127: What does WindowsAuthenticationModule do?

Answer:

The WindowsAuthenticationModule performs Windows Authentication and it can be set to active when the <authentication> module in the web.config file is set to: <authentication mode="Windows" />.

128: What does the PassportAuthenticationModule do?

Answer:

The PassportAuthenticationModule is active when the <authentication> element is set to Passport mode. It provides a wrapper for Microsoft's passport authentication service.

129: Which are the modules built for implementing Authorization?

Answer:

There are two modules built for implementing Authorization:

    a) UrlAuthorization and

    b) FileAuthorization.

130: What does UrlAuthorization do?

Answer:

UrlAuthorization restricts access to files and directories based on the user's name or the roles that are assigned to a user.

131: What does FileAuthorization do?

Answer:

FileAuthorization restricts access to files accessed by ASP.NET based on WindowsACLs.

PROFILES and ASP.NET

132: What are Profiles?

Answer:

Profiles store individual records identified by a unique user name. They oblige the user to use an authentication system which results in them receiving the unique user name.

133: What does the SqlProfileProvider do?

Answer:

The SqlProfileProvider allows for storing of profile information onto a SQL Server 7.0 or later. Also, the user has the option of creating profile tables in any database.

134: How are Profile Tables created?

Answer:

Profile tables are created using the aspnet_regsql.exe command with the –A command.

135: How can Profile properties be defined and how are they used?

Answer:

Profile properties need to be defined specifically by adding the <properties> element inside the <profile> section of the web.config file. They can be used by adding an authorization rule to prevent undesired access for the folder or page where the user wishes to use the profile.

136: How can a custom class be used with profiles?

Answer:

This process is easy to do and it requires the creation of a class that wraps the needed information allowing for use inside the class of public member variables or property procedures.

CRYPTOGRAPHY and .NET CRYPTOGRAPHY CLASSES

137: What is Cryptography?

Answer:

Cryptography is the art of scrambling data to ensure that confidentiality is kept and adding HASH codes to detect data tampering.

138: What does Hashing mean?

Answer:

Hashing is the storing of a digital fingerprint of original data and not the data itself. Because of this new original data cannot be reverse-hashed.

139: How many layers of encryption can we find in .NET?

Answer:

.NET's encryption classes are divided into three layers/ which in turn are separated into subclasses.

140: What does the first layer of encryption comprise of?

Answer:

The first layer is just a set of abstract base classes that represent an encryption task; these are: AsymmetricalAlgorithm; SymmetricalAlgorithm and HashAlgorithm.

141: What does the second layer of encryption comprise of?
Answer:
The second layer is formed out of classes that represent a specific encryption algorithm. They derive from the encryption base classes but are also abstract classes.

142: What does the third layer of encryption comprise of?
Answer:
The third layer is just a set of encryption implementations. Each implementation derives from an algorithm class.

143: What do symmetric algorithms do?
Answer:
Symmetric algorithms use the same key for encryption or decryption. Data encrypted with a key can only be decrypted

using the same key.

144: What do asymmetrical algorithms do?

Answer:

Asymmetrical algorithms solve some of the problems that symmetrical algorithms have by requiring different keys for encrypting and decrypting. These keys are called public keys and are handed to anyone that wishes to send encrypted information to the user.

THE CONTROL STATE

and DESIGN

145: What is the View state?

Answer:

View state is a property used to store and retrieve information that belongs to a web page. It is also used to retrieve private information after a postback.

146: What is the Control state?

Answer:

Control state is a feature used for storing data that a control misses. It works almost the same way View state does, but it is not affected by the EnableViewState property.

147: What do Attributes do?

Answer:

Attributes allow for a way to add information that relates to a piece of code without making the user change the code or create a separate file in a different format.

148: What does the Browsable(true|false) attribute do?

Answer:

If false, this property will not display in the Properties window. It is used to hide properties that cannot be changed at the design time.

149: What is Category(string)?

Answer:

It is a string that indicates the category under which the property will appear in the Properties window.

150: What is DefaulValue()?

Answer:

It is an attribute that sets the default value that will be shown for the property in the Properties window.

151: What does the MergableProperty(bool) do?

Answer:

This property configures how the Properties window behaves when more than one instance of this control is selected at once.

152: What does the RefreshProperties() do?

Answer:

It specifies if the rest of the Properties must be updated when this property is changed.

153: What does the DefaultEvent(string) do?

Answer:

It shows the name the default event. When double clicking the control on the design interface, Visual Studio adds an event handler for that event.

154: What does the DefaultProperty(string) do?

Answer:

It indicates the name of the default property that is highlighted in the Properties window the first time the control is selected.

155: What does the ControlValuePropertyAttribute(string) do?

Answer:

It indicates the name of the property that should be used by default when binding a control parameter to this control for use in the data source.

156: What does nonVisualControl() do?

Answer:

It indicates that this control has no runtime appearance.

157: What does TagPrefix(string, string) do?

Answer:

It associates a namespace with a prefix that will be used when adding control tags on an .aspx page.

158: What does ToolboxBitmap(type, string) do?

Answer:

It specifies the Bitmap that will be shown for this control when it is added to the Toolbox.

159: What does ToolboxData(string) do?

Answer:

It specifies the tag that will be created for this control in the .aspx file when the user drags it from the Toolbox.

160: How can a resource be retrieved?

Answer:

To retrieve a resource the user must tell the WebResource.axd handler what resource it needs and what assembly contains that resource.

161: What does the DesignerSerializationVisibility attribute do?

Answer:

This attribute determines if a property needs to be serialized by one of these three choices: visible, content and hidden.

162: What does the Persistence mode attribute do?

Answer:

It allows the user to specify how a property is serialized by using one of these choices: Attribute, InnerProperty, InnerDefaulProperty and EncodedInnerDefaultProperty.

163: What does GetEditStyle() do?

Answer:

It specifies if the type of editor is a DropDown (provides a list of drawn choices), Modal (provides a dialog box for property selection) or None (no editing is needed).

ImageMap CONTROL

in ASP.NET and GDI+

164: What are stacked image controls used for?

Answer:

They are used to make multiple borderless pictures look like one graphic when positioned one next to each other.

165: What does the ImageButton do?

Answer:

When it is clicked, it provides coordinates where the click has been made. It is however a technique prone to a lot of bugs.

166: What does the ImageMap control do?

Answer:

The ImageMap control is used to define separate regions by giving each one a separate name. It is mainly used for images that have small hotspots.

167: What is GDI+?

Answer:

GDI+ is a drawing model for ASP.NET applications that can

write documents to printers, display graphics in Windows applications and rendering graphics in a web page.

168: What is the System.Drawing.Graphics class?

Answer:

The Graphic class is a feature that uses a GDI+ drawing surface used as a last resort by developers who need to paint windows or print documents.

169: What do the DrawArc(), DrawBrezier() and so on methods do?

Answer:

These methods draw different shapes depending on the command used by the user. For example DrawArc() draws an arc representing a portion of an eclipse.

170: What does the FillEclipse() do?

Answer:

The method FillEclipse() fills the interior of an eclipse.

AJAX in ASP.NET

171: How many methods in AJAX library are used to pass information to event handlers?

Answer:

There are two methods that the ASP.NET AJAX library uses to pass additional information onto event handlers:

   a) Function.createCallback(method, context)

   b) Function.createDelegate(instance, method).

172: What does calling the createCallback() method do?

Answer:

This method creates a method that passes content parameters to the event handlers, like a string or a reference.

173: What does calling the createDelegate() method do?

Answer:

This method does not pass any additional parameters to the event handlers but changes the meaning of *this* in the handler. It makes *this* refer to anything the user wishes for.

174: How many versions of MicrosoftAjax.js file does the Ajax Library contain?

Answer:

There are two versions of the MicrosoftAjax.js file: the Release version and the Debug version

175: What is the Release version of the MicrosoftAjax.js file?

Answer:

The Release version is the simpler of the two and is a library minimized to its smallest size with all code and comments stripped.

176: What is the Debug version of the MicrosoftAjax.js file?

Answer:

The Debug version is pretty much readable and contains comments of the two methods. It also contains code needed to inform the user when he is misusing a method.

177: What does the Sys.Debug class in the Microsoft AJAX

Library do?

Answer:

This class is used to output trace messages and break into the Visual Web Developer debugger. It supports the following five methods: assert, clearTrace, fail, trace and traceDump.

178: Does ASP.NET AJAX provide support for calling web services?

Answer:

Yes. The user can call a web method from a separate web service or call a method that is exposed by the web page itself.

179: What is the QuotationService class?

Answer:

This class is the proxy class that is generated by the ServiceReference included in the ScriptManager control. It includes a method that corresponds to each of the remote web methods that are exposed by the web service.

180: What does the addMovie() method do?

Answer:

This method creates a new object that is named movietoAdd. This represents the values that the user has entered into the <input> elements of the txtTitle and txtDirector.

181: How many parameters does the AuthenticationService.login() method support?

Answer:

This method supports eight parameters and these are:

    a) userName,

    b) password,

    c) isPersistent,

    d) customInfo,

    e) redirectUrl,

    f) loginCompletedCallback,

    g) failedCallback and

    h) userContext.

182: What does the RoleService.load() method do?

Answer:

This method loads all the roles for the current user and it accepts two parameters: the method to call if the web service call is successful and the method to call if the web service call fails.

183: How many parameters does the $create() shortcut support?

Answer:

This method supports five parameters which are: type, properties, events, references and element.

184: Which are the methods needed to implement to the IScriptControl interface?

Answer:

The two methods needed are the GetScriptreferences() method and the GetScriptDescriptors() method.

185: What is a ScriptControl class and how many methods can it implement?

Answer:

The ScriptControl class is an abstract class and it can implement two methods: GetScriptreferences() and GetScriptDescriptors().

186: How can an extender control be created?

Answer:

An extender control can be created by either implementing the IExtenderControl interface or by deriving a control from the base ExtenderControl class.

MISCELLANEOUS

187: What is data binding in .NET?

Answer:

Data binding is a way that is used to connect values from a collection of data to the controls of a web form. The values are displayed in the controls without the user having to write separate code to display them.

188: How many directives can we find in ASP.NET?

Answer:

There are seven types of directives (in no particular order). They are:

a) reference,

b) assembly,

c) OutputCache,

d) register,

e) implements,

f) page and

g) import directives

189: What is CLR in ASP.NET?

Answer:

CLR means Common Language Runtime and it is a run time environment that manages the execution of the .NET code while providing services like debugging.

190: Which are the stages of a page load cycle in ASP.NET?

Answer:

The number of a page load cycle is comprised of four stages: Init(), Load(), PreRender() and Unload().

191: What does CLI mean in .NET?

Answer:

CLI is a set of applications for a runtime environment and it comprises of common type systems, a base class library and a CIL.

192: What does DLL Hell mean in ASP.NET?

Answer:

DLL Hell is a problem that occurs when the installation of a new application hinders other applications as new DLLs are copied into the system as older applications are not compatible with them.

193: What does Server.Transfer do?

Answer:

Server.Transfer tells the browser that the page the user is seeking can be found at a new location allowing the browser to initiate a new request.

194: What does Response.Redirect do?

Answer:

Response.Redirect transfers execution from the first page to a second page on the server, allowing any strings or variables to be made available to the second page as well.

195: What are Namespaces?

Answer:

Namespaces are the logical groupings of names that are used in a program. Multiple namespaces can appear in a single application code but the name of any given identifier must appear only once in its namespace.

196: What do the CheckBoxList and RadioButtonList do in ASP.NET 4?

Answer:

These controls now follow new values for the Repeatlayout property and these are: OrderedList and UnorderedList.

197: What happens when the GridView control is in edit mode?

Answer:

When in edit mode, the GridView makes use of Dynamic Data that validates that the entered data is in a proper format. If it is not, then an error message is displayed.

198: What does routing do in ASP.NET 4?

Answer:

Routing allows the user to configure an application to accept the request URLs that do not map to physical files and it makes use of the following features:

a) PageRouteHandler class,

b) HttpRequest.RequestContext and Page.RouteData properties,

c) RouteUrl, RouteValue and RouteParameter classes.

199: What are Areas in .NET?

Answer:

Areas allow the user to group controllers and views into sections of a massive application in relative isolation of other sections of a website with ease.

200: What does MVC do in .NET?

Answer:

MVC means Model View Controller and it is a design pattern meant for users to achieve the decoupling of data access from a presentation code allowing the users to test the GUI without having to make any if at all changes to it.

HR Questions

Review these typical interview questions and think about how you would answer them. Read the answers listed; you will find best possible answers along with strategies and suggestions.

This page is intentionally left blank

1: Tell me about yourself?

Answer:

The most often asked question in interviews. You need to have a short statement prepared in your mind. Keep your answer to one or two minutes. Don't ramble. Be careful that it does not sound rehearsed. Limit it to work-related items unless instructed otherwise. Talk about things you have done and jobs you have held that relate to the position you are interviewing for. Start with the item farthest back and work up to the present (If you have a profile or personal statement(s) at the top of your CV use this as your starting point).

2: Why did you leave your last job?

Answer:

Stay positive regardless of the circumstances. Never refer to a major problem with management and never speak ill of supervisors, co- workers or the organization. If you do, you will be the one looking bad. Keep smiling and talk about leaving for a positive reason such as an opportunity, a chance to do something special or other forward- looking reasons.

3: What experience do you have in this field?

Answer:

Speak about specifics that relate to the position you are applying for. If you do not have specific experience, get as close as you can.

4: Do you consider yourself successful?

Answer:

You should always answer yes and briefly explain why. A good explanation is that you have set goals, and you have met some and are on track to achieve the others.

5: What do co-workers say about you?

Answer:

Be prepared with a quote or two from co-workers. Either a specific statement or a paraphrase will work. Bill Smith, a co-worker at Clarke Company, always said I was the hardest worker' she had ever known. It should be as powerful as Bill having said it at the interview herself.

6: What do you know about this organization?

Answer:

This question is one reason to do some research on the organization before the interview. Research the company's products, size, reputation, Image, goals, problems, management style, skills, History and philosophy. Be informed and interested. Find out where they have been and where they are going. What are the current issues and who are the major players?

7: What have you done to improve your knowledge in the last year?

Answer:

Try to include improvement activities that relate to the job. A wide variety of activities can be mentioned as positive self-improvement. Have some good ones handy to mention.

8: Are you applying for other jobs?

Answer:

Be honest but do not spend a lot of time in this area. Keep the focus on this job and what you can do for this organization. Anything else is a distraction.

9: Why do you want to work for this organization?

Answer:

This may take some thought and certainly, should be based on the research you have done on the organization. Sincerity is extremely important here and will easily be sensed. Relate it to your long-term career goals. Never talk about what you want; first talk about their Needs. You want to be part of an exciting forward-moving company. You can make a definite contribution to specific company goals.

10: Do you know anyone who works for us?

Answer:

Be aware of the policy on relatives working for the organization. This can affect your answer even though they asked about friends not relatives. Be careful to mention a friend only if they are well thought of.

11: What kind of salary do you need?

Answer:

A loaded question! A nasty little game that you will probably lose if you answer first. So, do not answer it. Instead, say something like/ that's a tough question. Can you tell me the range for this position? In most cases, the interviewer, taken off guard, will tell you. If not, say that it can depend on the details of the job. Then give a wide range.

12: Are you a team player?

Answer:

You are, of course, a team player. Be sure to have examples ready. Specifics that show you often perform for the good of the team rather than for yourself is good evidence of your team attitude. Do not brag; just say it in a matter-of-fact tone. This is a key point.

13: How long would you expect to work for us if hired?

Answer:

Specifics here are not good. Something like this should work:

I'd like it to be a long time. Or As long as we both feel I'm doing a good job.

14: Have you ever had to fire anyone? How did you feel about that?

Answer:

This is serious. Do not make light of it or in any way seem like you like to fire people. At the same time, you will do it when it is the right thing to do. When it comes to the organization versus the individual who has created a harmful situation, you will protect the organization. Remember firing is not the same as layoff or reduction in force.

15: What is your philosophy towards work?

Answer:

The interviewer is not looking for a long or flowery dissertation here. Do you have strong feelings that the job gets done? Yes. That's the type of answer that works best here. Keep it short and positive, showing a benefit to the organization.

16: If you had enough money to retire right now, would you?

Answer:

Answer yes if you would. But since you need to work, this is the type of work you prefer. Do not say yes if you do not mean it.

17: Have you ever been asked to leave a position?

Answer:

If you have not, say no. If you have, be honest, brief and avoid saying negative things about the people or organization involved.

18: Explain how you would be an asset to this organization.

Answer:

You should be anxious for this question. It gives you a chance to highlight your best points as they relate to the position being discussed. Give a little advance thought to this relationship.

19: Why should we hire you?

Answer:

Point out how your assets meet what the organization needs. Also mention about your knowledge, experience, abilities, and skills. Never mention any other candidates to make a comparison.

20: Tell me about a suggestion you have made.

Answer:

Have a good one ready. Be sure and use a suggestion that was accepted and was then considered successful. One related to the type of work applied for is a real plus.

21: What irritates you about co-workers?

Answer:

This is a trap question. Think real hard but fail to come up with anything that irritates you. A short statement that you seem to get along with folks is great.

22: What is your greatest strength?

Answer:

Numerous answers are good, just stay positive. A few good

examples: Your ability to prioritize, Your problem-solving skills, Your ability to work under pressure, Your ability to focus on projects, Your professional expertise, Your leadership skills, Your positive attitude

23: Tell me about your dream job or what are you looking for in a job?
Answer:
Stay away from a specific job. You cannot win. If you say the job you are contending for is it, you strain credibility. If you say another job is it, you plant the suspicion that you will be dissatisfied with this position if hired. The best is to stay genetic and say something like: A job where I love the work, like the people, can contribute and can't wait to get to work.

24: Why do you think you would do well at this job?
Answer:
Give several reasons and include skills, experience and interest.

25: What do you find the most attractive about this position?

(Least attractive?)

Answer:

a) List a couple of attractive factors such as the responsibility the post offers and the opportunity to work with experienced teams that have a reputation for innovation and creativity.

b) Say you'd need more information and time before being able to make a judgment on any unattractive aspects.

26: What kind of person would you refuse to work with?

Answer:

Do not be trivial. It would take disloyalty to the organization, violence or lawbreaking to get you to object. Minor objections will label you as a whiner.

27: What is more important to you: the money or the work?

Answer:

Money is always important, but the work is the most important. There is no better answer.

28: What would your previous supervisor say your strongest point is?

Answer:

There are numerous good possibilities:

Loyalty, Energy, Positive attitude, Leadership, Team player, Expertise, Initiative, Patience, Hard work, Creativity, Problem solver.

29: Tell me about a problem you had with a supervisor.

Answer:

Biggest trap of all! This is a test to see if you will speak ill of your boss. If you fall for it and tell about a problem with a former boss, you may well below the interview right there. Stay positive and develop a poor memory about any trouble with a supervisor.

30: What has disappointed you about a job?

Answer:

Don't get trivial or negative. Safe areas are few but can include: Not enough of a challenge. You were laid off in a reduction

Company did not win a contract, which would have given you more responsibility.

31: Tell me about your ability to work under pressure.

Answer:

You may say that you thrive under certain types of pressure. Give an example that relates to the type of position applied for.

32: Do your skills match this job or another job more closely?

Answer:

Probably this one! Do not give fuel to the suspicion that you may want another job more than this one.

33: What motivates you to do your best on the job?

Answer:

This is a personal trait that only you can say, but good examples are: Challenge, Achievement, and Recognition.

34: Are you willing to work overtime? Nights? Weekends?

Answer:

This is up to you. Be totally honest.

35: How would you know you were successful on this job?

Answer:

Several ways are good measures:

You set high standards for yourself and meet them. Your outcomes are a success. Your boss tells you that you are successful and doing a great job.

36: Would you be willing to relocate if required?

Answer:

You should be clear on this with your family prior to the interview if you think there is a chance it may come up. Do not say yes just to get the job if the real answer is no. This can create a lot of problems later on in your career. Be honest at this point. This will save you from future grief.

37: Are you willing to put the interests of the organization ahead of your own?

Answer:

This is a straight loyalty and dedication question. Do not worry about the deep ethical and philosophical implications. Just say yes.

38: Describe your management style.

Answer:

Try to avoid labels. Some of the more common labels, like progressive, salesman or consensus, can have several meanings or descriptions depending on which management expert you listen to. The situational style is safe, because it says you will manage according to the situation, instead of one size fits all.

39: What have you learned from mistakes on the job?

Answer:

Here you have to come up with something or you strain credibility. Make it small, well intentioned mistake with a positive lesson learned. An example would be, working too far ahead of colleagues on a project and thus throwing coordination off.

40: Do you have any blind spots?

Answer:

Trick question! If you know about blind spots, they are no longer blind spots. Do not reveal any personal areas of concern here. Let them do their own discovery on your bad points. Do not hand it to them.

41: If you were hiring a person for this job, what would you look for?

Answer:

Be careful to mention traits that are needed and that you have.

42: Do you think you are overqualified for this position?

Answer:

Regardless of your qualifications, state that you are very well qualified for the position you've been interviewed for.

43: How do you propose to compensate for your lack of experience?

Answer:

First, if you have experience that the interviewer does not know about, bring that up: Then, point out (if true) that you are a hard working quick learner.

44: What qualities do you look for in a boss?

Answer:

Be generic and positive. Safe qualities are knowledgeable, a sense of humor, fair, loyal to subordinates and holder of high standards. All bosses think they have these traits.

45: Tell me about a time when you helped resolve a dispute between others.

Answer:

Pick a specific incident. Concentrate on your problem solving technique and not the dispute you settled.

46: What position do you prefer on a team working on a project?

Answer:

Be honest. If you are comfortable in different roles, point that out.

47: Describe your work ethic.

Answer:

Emphasize benefits to the organization. Things like, determination to get the job done and work hard but enjoy your work are good.

48: What has been your biggest professional disappointment?

Answer:

Be sure that you refer to something that was beyond your control. Show acceptance and no negative feelings.

49: Tell me about the most fun you have had on the job.

Answer:

Talk about having fun by accomplishing something for the organization.

50: What would you do for us? (What can you do for us that someone else can't?)

a) Relate past experiences that represent success in Working for your previous employer.

b) Talk about your fresh perspective and the relevant experience you can bring to the company.

c) Highlight your track record of providing creative, Workable solutions.

51: Do you have any questions for me?

Answer:

Always have some questions prepared. Questions prepared where you will be an asset to the organization are good. How soon will I be able to be productive? What type of projects will I be able to assist on?, are few examples.

And Finally Good Luck!

INDEX

ASP.NET

INTRODUCTION TO ASP.NET

1: How many types of ASP.NET are currently released?
2: What does ASP.NET 2.0 improve over the previous version?
3: What does ASP.NET AJAX do?
4: What is LINQ and what does it do?
5: Do current web browsers support ASP.NET 3.5? What is the role of ASP.NET in web development?
6: Is ASP.NET 3.5 a full ASP.NET version?
7: How do you add ASP.NET into a web site?

WEB FORMS and OBJECTS

8: What are web forms and what do they do?
9: What is page processing?
10: How are controls handled in ASP.NET?
11: What is the ASP.NET event model?
12: How do the events in ASP.NET function?
13: What is the view state mechanism in ASP.NET?
14: Does ASP.NET follow the rules of XHTML?
15: How does the user code initialize?
16: Does ASP.NET include validation controls?
17: What is the Response object in ASP.NET?
18: What is the Server object?
19: What is the User object?
20: What is the Trace object?

SERVER CONTROLS, OBJECTS and METHODS

21: What are server controls in ASP.NET?
22: How many types of server controls does ASP.NET allow?
23: What is the HTML server control class and what does it do?
24: What is the WebControl class and what does it do?
25: What is the Page class and what does it do?
26: What is the Session object?
27: What is the Application object?
28: What is the Cache object?
29: What is the Request object?
30: What is the Response object?

31: What is a Server object?
32: What is the Transfer() method?
33: What is the MapPath() method?
34: What is the HtmlEncode() method?
35: What is the User object?
36: What is the Trace object?

ASP.NET DATA BINDING

37: What does Data binding do in ASP.NET?
38: What are data source controls?
39: What is Basic Data Binding?
40: What does the Single Value Binding do?
41: What does the Repeated Value Binding do?
42: What does Data Source Controls comprise of?
43: What does the SqlDataSource do?
44: What does the ObjectDataSource do?

DATA CONTROLS and CACHING

45: What is the GridView control?
46: What is the ListView control?
47: What does the DetailsView do in ASP.NET?
48: What does the FormView do in ASP.NET?
49: What is Caching?
50: How many types of caching can we find in ASP.NET?
51: What does output caching do?
52: What does data caching do?
53: How can portions of a web page be cached?
54: How can fragment caching be implemented?
55: What is Post-Cache substitution?
56: What does cache configuration do?
57: What does cache priority do and what is it used for?

STREAMS and FILES

58: What do DirectoryInfo and FileInfo classes do?
59: What does the DriveInfo do?
60: How can File Version Information be retrieved?
61: What does the Path class do?
62: What are streams in ASP.NET?
63: How can text files be implemented with ASP.NET?
64: How can binary files be implemented in ASP.NET?

65: How can files be uploaded into ASP.NET?
66: What happens when a file bigger than 4MB is uploaded into ASP.NET?
67: What does compression do in ASP.NET?
68: How is compression used in ASP.NET?
69: What does Serialization do in ASP.NET?

LINQ

70: What is LINQ?
71: How do LINQ expressions work?
72: What do Grouping and Aggregation do in LINQ?
73: What are extension methods in LINQ?
74: What happens when LINQ to DataSet is used?
75: What are Typed DataSets in LINQ?
76: What does using LINQ to SQL result in?
77: What does DataContext do?
78: What does LinqDataSource do?

XML in ASP.NET

79: What is XML?
80: What are the advantages of using XML?
81: What is a Schema in XML?
82: How can a XML file be written?
83: What are the strategies of reading XML files?
84: What is a node in XML?
85: What does the XPath Navigator class do?
86: What does the XDocument do and what is its function?
87: How can XML content be read with XDocument?
88: How can XML content be searched?
89: How is XML content transforming achieved?
90: What does XML Control do?
91: What is the purpose of using XSLT?

USER CONTROLS

92: What are user controls in .NET?
93: What are custom server controls in .NET?
94: What do user controls comprise of?
95: How can a user control be created?
96: How can code be added to a user control?
97: How are dynamic user controls added?

THEMES in ASP.NET

98: What are themes in ASP.NET?
99: What are master pages in ASP.NET?
100: How can a Stylesheet be created?
101: What are Stylesheets used for?
102: How are Stylesheet rules applied?
103: Where are themes placed in a web application?
104: How can a Stylesheet be used as part of a theme?
105: What are HTML frames?

WEBSITES and NAVIGATION

106: What is the MultiView Control?
107: What is the Wizard control?
108: What is XmlSiteMapProvider?
109: What is SiteMapPath?
110: How can URL mapping be achieved?
111: What is the TreeView control?
112: What does the TreeNode do?
113: How many modes does TreeNode have?
114: What does the Menu Control do?
115: What does the MenuItem class do?

SECURITY in ASP.NET

116: What is Authentication in ASP.NET?
117: How do users prove their identity?
118: How many types of authentications does ASP.NET provide?
119: What is Impersonation?
120: What is Authorization?
121: What is Confidentiality?
122: What is Integrity?
123: What is Encryption?
124: How is Authentication handled in ASP.NET?
125: How many modules does ASP.NET use?
126: What does FormsAuthenticationModule do?
127: What does WindowsAuthenticationModule do?
128: What does the PassportAuthenticationModule do?
129: Which are the modules built for implementing Authorization?
130: What does UrlAuthorization do?
131: What does FileAuthorization do?

PROFILES and ASP.NET

132: What are Profiles?
133: What does the SqlProfileProvider do?
134: How are Profile Tables created?
135: How can Profile properties be defined and how are they used?
136: How can a custom class be used with profiles?

CRYPTOGRAPHY and .NET CRYPTOGRAPHY CLASSES

137: What is Cryptography?
138: What does Hashing mean?
139: How many layers of encryption can we find in .NET?
140: What does the first layer of encryption comprise of?
141: What does the second layer of encryption comprise of?
142: What does the third layer of encryption comprise of?
143: What do symmetric algorithms do?
144: What do asymmetrical algorithms do?

THE CONTROL STATE and DESIGN

145: What is the View state?
146: What is the Control state?
147: What do Attributes do?
148: What does the Browsable(true | false) attribute do?
149: What is Category(string)?
150: What is DefaulValue()?
151: What does the MergableProperty(bool) do?
152: What does the RefreshProperties() do?
153: What does the DefaultEvent(string) do?
154: What does the DefaultProperty(string) do?
155: What does the ControlValuePropertyAttribute(string) do?
156: What does nonVisualControl() do?
157: What does TagPrefix(string, string) do?
158: What does ToolboxBitmap(type, string) do?
159: What does ToolboxData(string) do?
160: How can a resource be retrieved?
161: What does the DesignerSerializationVisibility attribute do?
162: What does the Persistence mode attribute do?
163: What does GetEditStyle() do?

ImageMap CONTROL in ASP.NET and GDI+

164: What are stacked image controls used for?

165: What does the ImageButton do?
166: What does the ImageMap control do?
167: What is GDI+?
168: What is the System.Drawing.Graphics class?
169: What do the DrawArc(), DrawBrezier() and so on methods do?
170: What does the FillEclipse() do?

AJAX in ASP.NET

171: How many methods in AJAX library are used to pass information to event handlers?
172: What does calling the createCallback() method do?
173: What does calling the createDelegate() method do?
174: How many versions of MicrosoftAjax.js file does the Ajax Library contain?
175: What is the Release version of the MicrosoftAjax.js file?
176: What is the Debug version of the MicrosoftAjax.js file?
177: What does the Sys.Debug class in the Microsoft AJAX Library do?
178: Does ASP.NET AJAX provide support for calling web services?
179: What is the QuotationService class?
180: What does the addMovie() method do?
181: How many parameters does the AuthenticationService.login() method support?
182: What does the RoleService.load() method do?
183: How many parameters does the $create() shortcut support?
184: Which are the methods needed to implement to the IScriptControl interface?
185: What is a ScriptControl class and how many methods can it implement?
186: How can an extender control be created?

MISCELLANEOUS

187: What is data binding in .NET?
188: How many directives can we find in ASP.NET?
189: What is CLR in ASP.NET?
190: Which are the stages of a page load cycle in ASP.NET?
191: What does CLI mean in .NET?
192: What does DLL Hell mean in ASP.NET?
193: What does Server.Transfer do?
194: What does Response.Redirect do?
195: What are Namespaces?
196: What do the CheckBoxList and RadioButtonList do in ASP.NET 4?
197: What happens when the GridView control is in edit mode?
198: What does routing do in ASP.NET 4?
199: What are Areas in .NET?
200: What does MVC do in .NET?

HR Questions

1: Tell me about yourself?
2: Why did you leave your last job?
3: What experience do you have in this field?
4: Do you consider yourself successful?
5: What do co-workers say about you?
6: What do you know about this organization?
7: What have you done to improve your knowledge in the last year?
8: Are you applying for other jobs?
9: Why do you want to work for this organization?
10: Do you know anyone who works for us?
11: What kind of salary do you need?
12: Are you a team player?
13: How long would you expect to work for us if hired?
14: Have you ever had to fire anyone? How did you feel about that?
15: What is your philosophy towards work?
16: If you had enough money to retire right now, would you?
17: Have you ever been asked to leave a position?
18: Explain how you would be an asset to this organization.
19: Why should we hire you?
20: Tell me about a suggestion you have made.
21: What irritates you about co-workers?
22: What is your greatest strength?
23: Tell me about your dream job or what are you looking for in a job?
24: Why do you think you would do well at this job?
25: What do you find the most attractive about this position? (Least attractive?)
26: What kind of person would you refuse to work with?
27: What is more important to you: the money or the work?
28: What would your previous supervisor say your strongest point is?
29: Tell me about a problem you had with a supervisor.
30: What has disappointed you about a job?
31: Tell me about your ability to work under pressure.
32: Do your skills match this job or another job more closely?
33: What motivates you to do your best on the job?
34: Are you willing to work overtime? Nights? Weekends?
35: How would you know you were successful on this job?
36: Would you be willing to relocate if required?
37: Are you willing to put the interests of the organization ahead of your own?
38: Describe your management style.
39: What have you learned from mistakes on the job?

40: Do you have any blind spots?

41: If you were hiring a person for this job, what would you look for?

42: Do you think you are overqualified for this position?

43: How do you propose to compensate for your lack of experience?

44: What qualities do you look for in a boss?

45: Tell me about a time when you helped resolve a dispute between others.

46: What position do you prefer on a team working on a project?

47: Describe your work ethic.

48: What has been your biggest professional disappointment?

49: Tell me about the most fun you have had on the job.

50: What would you do for us? (What can you do for us that someone else can't?)

51: Do you have any questions for me?

Some of the following titles might also be handy:
1. Oracle / PLSQL Interview Questions
2. ASP.NET Interview Questions
3. VB.NET Interview Questions
4. .NET Framework Interview Questions
5. C#.NET Interview Questions
6. OOPS Interview Questions
7. Core Java Interview Questions
8. JSP-Servlet Interview Questions
9. EJB (J2EE) Interview Questions
10. ADO.NET Interview Questions
11. SQL Server Interview Questions
12. C & C++ Interview Questions
13. 200 (HR) Interview Questions
14. JavaScript Interview Questions
15. JAVA/J2EE Interview Questions
16. Oracle DBA Interview Questions
17. XML Interview Questions
18. UNIX Shell Programming Interview Questions
19. PHP Interview Questions
20. J2ME Interview Questions
21. Hardware and Networking Interview Questions
22. Data Structures & Algorithms Interview Questions
23. Oracle E-Business Suite Interview Questions
24. UML Interview Questions
25. HTML, XHTML & CSS Interview Questions
26. JDBC Interview Questions
27. Hibernate, Springs & Struts Interview Questions
28. Linux Interview Questions

For complete list visit
www.vibrantpublishers.com

NOTES

CPSIA information can be obtained at www.ICGtesting.com
Printed in the USA
BVOW021751070212

282410BV00004B/5/P